The Care & Keeping of YOU Journal 2

for Older Girls

Cara Natterson, MD, Medical Consultant
Illustrated by Josée Masse

Published by American Girl Publishing
Copyright © 2013 American Girl

Questions or comments? Call 1-800-845-0005,
visit **americangirl.com,** or write to Customer Service,
American Girl, 8400 Fairway Place, Middleton, WI 53562-0497.

Printed in China
14 15 16 17 18 19 LEO 11 10 9 8 7 6 5 4 3

Editorial Development: Carrie Anton

Art Direction & Design: Camela Decaire

Production: Paula Moon, Kristi Tabrizi, Judith Lary,
Tami Kepler

Illustrations: Josée Masse

Medical consultant: Cara Natterson, MD

Note: Smart in Your Own Way and "Smarts Style" Decoder
are loosely based on Howard Gardner's "The Nine Types of
Intelligence."

Dear Reader,

The world is changing all around you—*and you're doing a lot of changing, too.* Sometimes you may feel as if your head is filled with tons of confusing questions. You have your mom, dad, teacher, coach, or other trusted adult to turn to for advice. But when you need to be alone with your thoughts, *The Care and Keeping of You 2 Journal* is here to be your guide.

Just as you did in *The Care and Keeping of You Journal,* this second journal offers the next step in writing about your thoughts, thinking about growing up, creating life lists, drawing yourself in your world, and so much more.

What you think and feel makes you special. This journal is the perfect place to celebrate all the unique things that make you the awesome individual you are!

Your friends at American Girl

I Bet You Didn't Know

Your family, friends, and important people in your life may think they know all about you, but there's always something that others would be surprised to learn. In response to the prompts below, write down something that others probably don't know about you.

My family might be surprised to know that I often think about

My teachers might be surprised to know

My friends might be surprised to know that I love to eat

My family might be surprised to know that I laugh really hard when

My mom might be surprised to know that my guilty pleasure is

My dad might be surprised to know that I love the sound of

Everyone might be surprised to know that my favorite

thing about myself is

Mental Match?

Does the body image in your mind match what you see in the mirror? It's not uncommon for people to think their bodies are different from what they really are. See how you shape up by drawing a full-body picture of yourself in the space below. On the next page, attach a full-body photograph of yourself. Then answer the questions that follow.

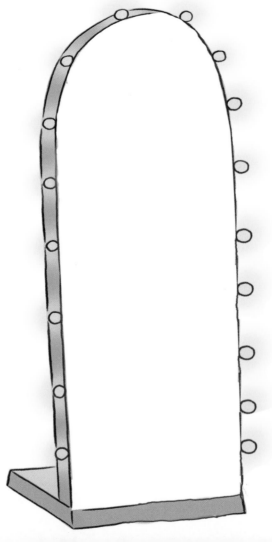

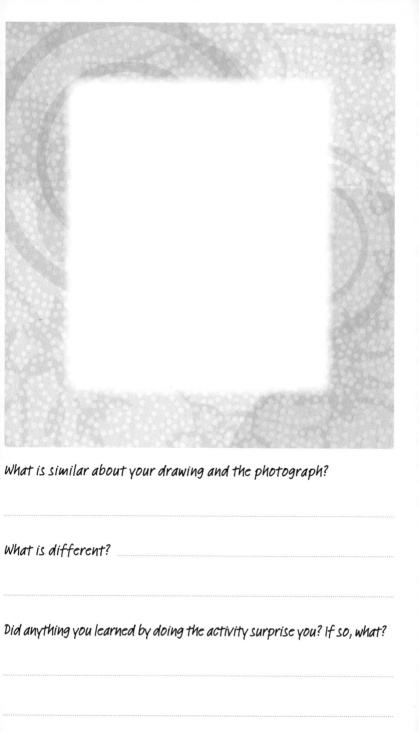

What is similar about your drawing and the photograph?

....

What is different? ....

....

Did anything you learned by doing the activity surprise you? If so, what?

....

....

Ready? Set? Goal!

If you've ever set a goal, you know how motivating it is to try to achieve it. Answer these goal-related questions. Then use the space provided to set a new goal.

Have you ever accomplished a goal you set?   Yes ☐   No ☐

If yes, what was the goal? ....

....

What steps did you take to achieve it? ....

....

....

What was the hardest part of setting your goal? ....

....

What was the hardest part of reaching your goal? ....

....

What did you learn that you would use the next time you

go for a goal? ....

....

....

Your new goal: ....

....

....

Why you set this goal: ....

....

....

I will complete this goal by (date/time) ....

People who can help me achieve my goal: ....

....

....

....

Goal Tips

1. Pick a goal that is meaningful to you. Don't just do something that you think your friends would like to do.

2. Set a goal that is specific. Instead of saying, "I want to be better in school," try, "I'm going to earn an A in math."

3. Make it something you DO instead of something you STOP doing. Instead of, "I'm going to stop watching so much TV," try, "I'm going to watch no more than 30 minutes of TV each day."

A Look-Up-To File

Think of some people—family, friends, or even famous people—whom you admire. List what makes each of them special.

Name: ....

I admire this person because ....

....

....

I can have good qualities like this person if I ....

....

Name: ....

I admire this person because ....

....

....

I can have good qualities like this person if I ....

....

....

Name: ....

I admire this person because ....
....
....
....

I can have good qualities like this person if I ....
....
....

Name: ....

I admire this person because ....
....
....

I can have good qualities like this person if I ....
....
....

Describe Your Day

Each day is different. Some days will be great, some will be so-so, and some might leave you down in the dumps. Throughout this journal, use the "Describe Your Day" pages to keep track of your activities and your feelings about various moments in time.

Date: ....

Today was a .... day.
(Fill in a word or phrase that best describes your day.)

What happened today: ....

....

....

....

....

How you feel about today: ....

....

What good things from today would you love to repeat?

....

....

....

What bad things from today would you choose to avoid?

....

....

....

What can you learn from today to make future days even better?

....

....

....

....

....

....

....

....

....

....

....

....

Food and Mood

What you eat sometimes affects how you feel. Use these pages to track your foods and feelings.

Monday

Breakfast

My mood:

Snack

My mood:

Lunch

My mood:

Tuesday

Breakfast

My mood:

Snack

My mood:

Lunch

My mood:

Wednesday

Breakfast

My mood:

Snack

My mood:

Lunch

My mood:

Thursday

Breakfast

My mood:

Snack

My mood:

Lunch

My mood:

Friday

Breakfast

My mood:

Snack

My mood:

Lunch

My mood:

Saturday

Breakfast

My mood:

Snack

My mood:

Lunch

My mood:

Sunday

Breakfast

My mood:

Snack

My mood:

Lunch

My mood:

Once you've completed the week, look for any patterns. Are you cranky mid-morning after skipping breakfast? Are you tired a few hours after eating a bag of candy? What changes could you make to feel better?

Snack

My mood:

Dinner

My mood:

Snack

My mood:

Snack

My mood:

Dinner

My mood:

Snack

My mood:

Snack

My mood:

Dinner

My mood:

Snack

My mood:

Snack

My mood:

Dinner

My mood:

Snack

My mood:

Snack

My mood:

Dinner

My mood:

Snack

My mood:

Snack

My mood:

Dinner

My mood:

Snack

My mood:

Snack

My mood:

Dinner

My mood:

Snack

My mood:

Life-Changing

With a few changes, your life could look a lot different than it does now!

If I had all the time I wanted, I'd

If I had all the money I could want, I'd

If I were the smartest person ever, I'd

If I had all the power in the world, I'd

If I had all the craft supplies I could imagine, I'd

If I could build a spaceship, I'd

If I were the fastest runner in the world, I'd

If I could create a new animal, I'd

If I could grow any kind of make-believe plant, I'd

If I could _____, I'd

Did It!

Create a list below of the coolest things you've ever done.

To-Do List

Create a list of some cool things you want to try.

No Two Are Equal

On these two pages, use a red pen to circle all the words that name things you can control. Use a blue pen to circle things that you cannot change. And use a green pen to circle things that change naturally over time. (Note: Some words may be circled with more than one color. And answers will differ depending on the person.)

sense of touch

muscle size

food

eye color

tastes

shoe size

sense of smell

clothing

knowledge

friendships

attitude

skills

sense of sight

hobbies

athletic ability

humor

complexion

home location

thoughts

height

emotions

sense of taste

weight

craft skills

interests

hair color

skin color

sense of hearing

heritage

school

language skills

Dare to Be Different

If you completed the activity on the last two pages, you probably have a better understanding of things you can control when it comes to your body and mind and things that are completely out of your hands. But what if you had the power to change some things? Use these prompts to create a new you—then draw a picture on the next page of what you'd look like.

"New Me" height: .... Why? ....

....

"New Me" hair color: .... Why? ....

....

"New Me" eye color: .... Why? ....

....

"New Me" attitude: .... Why? ....

....

"New Me" skills: .... Why? ....

....

How is the new you like the real you? ....

How is the new you different from the real you? ....

....

Why is being the real you better?

Non-Body Best

Draw a picture of your best quality that has nothing to do with your physical attributes. That means, don't draw a picture of your long, curly hair or your bright blue eyes.

What quality did you draw? ....

....

Was it easy to think of what to draw? Why or why not?

....

....

....

....

Is it easy or hard to draw something that you can't really see? Why?

....

....

....

....

....

....

....

....

Make a Motto

A *motto* is a statement of words to live by. It's a phrase you repeat to yourself when you want to stay focused, when you want to stick with your goal, or when you want to calm down. It should be a positive phrase that you really believe. Below are some examples of mottos. On the next page, write your own motto that is unique and has special meaning to you. Then say it to yourself whenever you need it!

I am creative.

Have the courage to take the first step.

I am smart.

I am the person I want to be.

What I say matters.

There is only one me.

Worrying gets me nowhere.

Make today amazing.

My life is a result of choices I make.

I believe I can.

I am my own best friend.

Go for it.

Being my best is about trying my hardest.

It's nice to be great, but it's great to be nice.

Keep it simple.

I am me.

I love being me.

I am enough.

Be happy.

Just breathe.

Make today the best day ever.

Every journey starts with the first step.

I am important.

Keep going.

It'll be OK.

I believe in myself.

Never give up.

I am grateful for this day.

Nobody's perfect.

I am special.

I can do anything.

My motto: ....

....

What it means to me: ....

....

....

Be Nice to Yourself

You most likely compliment other people often: "I love your braids!" "Cool T-shirt!" "Wow, those shoes are awesome!" And you probably go out of the way to be nice to other people: leaving a sweet note for your mom; helping your little brother with his homework; making a bracelet for your best friend. Do the same great things for yourself. In the space below, write six compliments about **you.** On the next page, write six things that you did for yourself today.

My compliments for me:

1. ....

....

2. ....

....

3. ....

....

4. ....

....

5. ....

....

6. ....

....

What I did for myself today:

1. ....

....

2. ....

....

3. ....

....

4. ....

....

5. ....

....

6. ....

....

Study Your Sleep

Day/Date	Time to Bed	Time Out of Bed	Time Asleep

On average, how many hours of sleep are you getting each night?

Growing bodies want at least ten hours of sleep each night. For one full week, use this chart to see if you're catching the ZZZs you need. Then answer the questions.

Awake Time	Sleep Notes	Morning Mood Why?

Do you need more sleep? If so, what can you do to get more?

_____

Describe Your Day

Keep track of your activities and your feelings about this
moment in time.

Date: ....

Today was a .... day.
(Fill in a word or phrase that best describes your day.)

What happened today: ....

....

....

....

....

How you feel about today: ....

....

What good things from today would you love to repeat?

....

....

....

....

What bad things from today would you choose to avoid?

....

....

....

What can you learn from today to make future days even better?

....

....

....

....

....

....

....

....

....

....

....

....

Mom and Me

These pages are all about you and the woman who knows you best—your mom!

Ways that Mom and I are most alike:

Ways that Mom and I are most different:

Things I love doing with Mom:

Good memories of Mom and me together:

Things I've always wanted to know about Mom:

Reasons that I love Mom:

TV Watching

A *stereotype* is a way of labeling a person according to a quality or trait that she has. For example, if someone is smart, she might be stereotyped as a nerd or a teacher's pet. If someone is pretty, she might be stereotyped as the popular girl. TV shows often portray these kinds of stereotypes using the characters they feature. Think of a show (or shows) you watch regularly, and see if you can spot any stereotypes at play.

Show title: ....

What is the show about? ....

....

Character name: ....

Describe the traits of this character (looks, clothing, attitude, intelligence, activities, number of friends, etc.).

....

....

Is this a stereotype? If so, what kind? ....

....

....

....

Character name: ....

Describe the traits of this character (looks, clothing, attitude, intelligence, activities, number of friends, etc.).

....

....

Is this a stereotype? If so, what kind? ....

....

....

....

Character name: ....

Describe the traits of this character (looks, clothing, attitude, intelligence, activities, number of friends, etc.).

....

....

Is this a stereotype? If so, what kind? ....

....

....

....

Zits Are the Pits

Circle the face that you think looks most like yours in terms of breakouts.

How many times a day do you wash your face? ....

How many days a week do you wash your face? ....

What kind of cleanser do you use? ....

Do you use a moisturizer? ....

What kind of moisturizer do you use? ....

Tip: Wash your face every morning and every night. If you exercise or play sports, also wash your face after you sweat. And remember to moisturize!

Having acne can make you feel as if people are staring at your spots. The good news is that they're not! Still, there are lots of things you can do to keep your skin clear. Answer the questions below to track your skin-care habits.

Now look in the mirror and circle the face that REALLY looks like you.

(Sometimes we make things worse in our mind than they really are!)

Do you wear cosmetics?

Tip: Oil-based facial products and makeup can make acne worse. To tame the zits, try water-based products instead.

Have you talked to your mom or dad about help they can give you to improve your skin?

Tip: Mom and Dad both went through puberty, so they understand how you feel and can offer help. If you think you're doing everything you can, it might be time to visit a doctor. A doctor can prescribe treatments when over-the-counter products aren't working.

Create a Collage

A *collage* is a work of art made up of different materials glued on a surface. Use the space on these pages to create a collage that represents female body image.

From magazines, cut out pictures of girls and women featured in articles and advertisements. Completely cover these two pages by gluing on the images. Once the entire space is filled, cover the magazine images with photos of your friends and female family members. Then turn the pages to answer questions about this activity.

Collage Questions

Once you've completed the "Create a Collage" activity, answer the following questions.

What kinds of magazines did you use to create your collage?

Was it easy or hard to find images of females in these magazines?

If you had to find one thing in common among the females from the magazines, what would it be?

Did you notice any major differences among the females from the magazines?

What did the images from the magazines have in common with

the photographs of your female friends and family members?

What were the differences?

Were you surprised by anything in this activity? If so, what?

Do you think magazines do a good or bad job of showing what an

"average" female looks like? Why?

Dad and Me

These pages are all about you and the man who knows you best—your dad!

Ways that Dad and I are most alike:

Ways that Dad and I are most different:

Things I love doing with Dad:

Good memories of Dad and me together: ....

....

....

....

....

Things I've always wanted to know about Dad: ....

....

....

....

Reasons that I love Dad: ....

....

....

....

....

Describe a Time When ..

Your feelings change all the time. Complete the phrases below to see for yourself.

Describe a time when you were proud of yourself.

....

....

....

How did it feel? ....

Describe a time when you hurt someone's feelings.

....

....

....

How did it feel? ....

Describe a time when someone said that you were smart.

....

....

....

How did it feel? ....

Describe a time when you were helpful to your community.

....

....

....

How did it feel?..

Describe a time when you were confident about trying something.

....

....

....

How did it feel?..

Describe a time when you stood up for yourself or someone else.

....

....

....

How did it feel?..

Smart in Your Own Way

While everyone can learn, each person learns best in her own way. Some people learn best from reading, whereas others learn best from doing. There are all kinds of ways to learn. To find out what your "smarts style" is, circle at least five words or phrases on these pages that best describe your strengths and interests. Then turn the page to read the results.

composing

storytelling

making collages

doing experiments

whistling

playing sports

looking for unique cloud shapes

working on group projects

teaching

playing musical instruments

thinking about my feelings

working with shapes

telling jokes

watching butterflies

doing sign language

playing on a team

doing crafts

doing yoga

solving math equations

drawing maps

keeping non-harmful secrets

sketching

remembering melodies

understanding charts and graphs

dream tracking

remembering information

going to parties

having quiet alone time

problem solving

miming

helping a friend with a problem

cheering up someone

taking nature hikes

journaling

listening

dancing

acting

reading

learning about animals

learning song lyrics

writing about my thoughts

organizing

camping

setting goals

singing

playing charades

learning definitions

listening to music

working jigsaw puzzles

growing plants

"Smarts Style" Decoder

Look at the colors of the words you circled on the previous two pages. Read the results below for the color circled most to see which kind of intelligence you have. If there is a tie, read both sections, because they both may apply to you.

If you circled more red words, you are **self smart.** You do your best learning when you go solo. The alone time gives you the chance to think deeply about how things work and how they relate to you. You don't need to be on your own all the time, but save playtime for friends and study time just for you.

If you circled more blue words, you are **people smart.** You love interacting with others and learning from group activities. When preparing for a big test, pull together a group of friends to study at your house. You'll have tons of fun and learn at the same time.

If you circled more orange words, you are **body smart.** Sitting still just isn't your thing. You prefer to be hands-on with what you're learning, and your body needs to be in motion to help new ideas sink in. To help you learn and remember, make up hand signs that match the facts. Then practice these over and over again. Muscle memory will help the hard stuff stick better in your brain.

If you circled more green words, you are **picture smart.** You have a visually artistic side, and this helps you learn. By seeing information through drawings, photographs, and charts, you're making mental images that are easy for you to remember. If the facts that you need to study don't come in the form of pictures, make your own!

If you circled more pink words, you are **logic smart.** When it's time to learn, you prefer numbers, formulas, and codes. You look at information as a puzzle, and then think through how to solve that puzzle. When it comes time to do homework, find ways to connect information through sequences and patterns.

If you circled more purple words, you are **music smart.** Rhythm and melodies easily stick in your mind, which makes them great tools to help you learn. When studying, make up rhymes and songs using the facts you need to remember. The tunes will be easy to recall when test time comes.

If you circled more turquoise words, you are **word smart.** For you, it's all about words, words, words. You learn best through reading, writing, and having discussions. To make the most of your learning time, crack open both your textbook and your notebook so that you can jot down facts as you find them.

If you circled more yellow words, you are **discovery smart.** Just like someone who is body smart, you learn best by being hands-on, but you prefer to do that outdoors. Call on your inner explorer to learn. Collecting, sorting, and comparing can be done with rocks, leaf specimens, and facts. While sitting outside, see how you become one with the subject you are studying.

Describe Your Day

Keep track of your activities and your feelings about this moment in time.

Date: ....

Today was a .... day.

(Fill in the word or phrase that best describes your day.)

What happened today: ....

....

....

....

....

How you feel about today: ....

....

What good things from today would you love to repeat?

....

....

....

....

What bad things from today would you choose to avoid?

_____

_____

_____

What can you learn from today to make future days even better?

_____

_____

_____

_____

_____

_____

_____

_____

_____

_____

_____

Period Tracker

Don't let your period come as a complete surprise.

When you first start getting your period, you won't always know precisely when it will arrive. That's because your period may not be regular in the beginning—instead of coming once a month, it might happen two weeks apart, then seven weeks apart, then three weeks apart. It's annoying, but you can learn your body's pattern by keeping track on a calendar, such as the one provided.

Each day you have your period, put an X in that day's box. Once your periods become regular, which usually happens within one to two years, they should last about the same length of time each month.

Timing Tips

- A period usually lasts about a week, but it can be longer or shorter and still be normal.
- The heaviest bleeding is usually during the first few days.
- Periods usually occur about every four weeks, counting from the first day of one period to the first day of the next period.

	jan	feb	mar	apr	may	jun	jul	aug	sep	oct	nov	dec
1												
2												
3												
4												
5												
6												
7												
8												
9												
10												
11												
12												
13												
14												
15												
16												
17												
18												
19												
20												
21												
22												
23												
24												
25												
26												
27												
28												
29												
30												
31												

Period Patterns

New moods and sensations may come when your period does.

During your period, or before your period starts, it's totally normal to feel crabby or achy—or both! The moody part has a lot to do with your changing hormone levels, whereas the body pains and cramps have to do with the shedding of your uterine lining. It's also completely normal to feel just the same as you always do.

Use the charts below to track how you feel.

My Body

	Achy	Tired	So-So	Comfortable	Energized
Before period	◯	◯	◯	◯	◯
During	◯	◯	◯	◯	◯
After	◯	◯	◯	◯	◯

Try It:
- If you have cramps, try wearing clothes that fit more loosely around your waist.
- When cramps are really bad, try sitting or lying down to help them go away.
- With help from an adult, try putting a heating pad on your lower belly when cramps are too much to handle.
- For cramps that are severe, talk to a parent about trying medicines that can help. Never take these without getting a parent's permission first.

My Mood

	Crabby	Sad	So-So	Happy	Psyched
Before period	◯	◯	◉	◯	◯
During	◯	◯	◉	◯	◯
After	◯	◯	◯	◯	◯

Try It:

- Give yourself a time-out.
- Take your anger out on something, not someone.
- Say you're sorry when needed.
- Make good choices.
- Get plenty of sleep.
- Talk it out with a trusted adult.

Outside Changes

You're great just the way you are, but that doesn't mean you can't try a new style or give yourself a new look. There are all kinds of ways to switch things up. Circle the things on these pages that you'd want to try.

Add a piece of jewelry to dress up an outfit.

Wear a scarf.

Change the laces in my sneakers.

Put my hair up.

Mix two different but coordinating patterns.

Wear colorful shoes.

Wear my hair down.

Wear a hat.

Wear a watch with a brightly colored band.

Grow my hair long.

Wear a pastel-colored top.

Wear a new hair accessory.

Braid my hair.

Add a contrasting belt to an outfit.

Wear a ribbon in my hair.

Wear contact lenses instead of glasses.

Wear mismatched, colorful socks.

Wear glasses.

Have my hair cut in a new style.

Wear three bracelets at the same time.

Add an embellishment to my flip-flops.

What's on the Inside

You may have heard the saying, "It's what's inside that counts." Well, it's true. But if you've had a rotten day and come off a little snippier than usual, you need to change your interior point of view. Just as on the last two pages, you'll find ways here to switch things up. But this time, the theme is changing the way you feel. Circle the things that you'd like to try. And the next time you need a mood change, flip back to these pages!

Help my mom or dad with dinner.

Write a poem.

Compliment another person.

Clean my room.

Draw a picture of myself.

Get some exercise.

Make a card for someone I know.

Read a book.

Drink a glass of water.

Write a story.

Talk to a parent.

Read a joke book.

Take a deep breath and count to 10.

Talk to a friend.   Watch a funny movie.

Go outside for fresh air.

Draw a picture of an animal.

Make a list of all that I am thankful for today.

Dance to a song.

Play with a pet.

Listen to my favorite music.

Work on a craft.

Play with a younger sibling or neighbor.

Love Is All Around You

Lots of people in your life love and care about you. Use these pages to draw pictures of four people you know who will support you when you need it.

Story of My Life

Everyone's life is different and unique. Use these pages to tell a part of your story!

EEK!

People are afraid of different things for many reasons. On these pages are some common fears, as well as a few that are less common. Circle any of the fears that you have had in the past or have now. Then answer the questions on the following pages.

open spaces

crowds

change

doctors

germs

needles

falling

water

birds

being alone

heights

thunderstorms

flying

dogs

failure

public speaking

cats

spiders

small spaces

snakes

taking tests

clowns

dentists

strangers

monsters

insects

the dark

Face Your Fears

Of course it's scary, but you CAN overcome things that make you feel afraid. Maybe you already have! If so, fill in the spaces below.

A fear I had when I was little but no longer have:

How the fear went away:

A time when I confronted my fear:

A time when a fear kept me from doing something:

How it made me feel: ....

....

....

....

Today, my biggest fear is ....

....

....

....

Advice I would give to a friend with a fear: ....

....

....

....

....

....

Been There

Below, try to list all the places you've ever visited.

Going There...One Day

Make a list below of places you'd love to see someday.

Describe Your Day

Keep track of your activities and your feelings about this moment in time.

Date: ....

Today was a .... day.
(Fill in a word or phrase that best describes your day.)

What happened today: ....

....

....

....

....

How you feel about today: ....

....

What good things from today would you love to repeat?

....

....

....

....

What bad things from today would you choose to avoid?

What can you learn from today to make future days even better?

Dream Outfit

Imagine and then draw a picture of your dream outfit below. On the next page, write a short story that features you wearing the outfit.

My story:

I Did It

Make a list below of some great things—big or small—that you've accomplished during your life.

Do-Over

Make a list below of things—big or small—that you've regretted doing and wish you could do over.

Class Act

Each semester in school means learning new things, having new experiences, and getting to know your student self a little better. Your next assignment is to answer the school-related questions below to create your very own progress report.

I am currently in .... grade.

I start school at .... a.m. and end school at .... p.m.

I sit next to .... and .... in .... class.

My favorite part about school is ....

....

This is my favorite because ....

....

....

The class I like the best is ....

....

I like this class because ....

....

....

....

The class I struggle with most is ....

....

That's because ....

....

....

If I could change anything about school, it would be ....

....

....

My grades are ....

My dream class would be ....

....

....

Extracurricular activities that I'm involved in include

....

....

....

....

....

Stressed Out

If you ever feel as if you're carrying a weight on your shoulders, you're probably stressed out. When stress gets you down, people may tell you to relax or chill out, but often that's not easy. *The Care and Keeping of You 2* offers tips to help you put aside stresses, and writing about them can help, too. Getting thoughts on paper might release them from swirling in your brain—and that is a good first step toward letting stress go.

Today, I'm stressed about

Here's what happened:

Why it's stressing me out:

The situation makes me feel

When stressful things happen, waiting is often the best way to feel better. Wait three to five days after you've filled out the preceding page. Then fill in the spaces below.

Today, I feel

Why I feel this way:

What I did or who I talked to about the stressful situation:

What I'll do next time I'm stressed:

What I learned about myself:

Friends Forever

You can count on a friend to lend a hand, listen to your embarrassing story, or give you a hug when you're feeling down. And to have a good friend, you must be a good friend in return. Next to each word below, give a specific example of how you carried out that action for or with a friend. If you don't have an example, it might be something you could work on to help your current friendships bloom.

Listened: ....

....

....

Helped: ....

....

....

Cheered: ....

....

....

Apologized: ....

....

....

Laughed: ....

....

....

Comforted: ....

....

....

Taught: ....

....

....

Compromised: ....

....

....

Supported: ....

....

....

Surprised: ....

....

....

Shape Up

To stay healthy, you need at least 60 minutes of exercise each day. That seems like a lot, but you don't have to do it all at once. And the more you exercise, the easier it should become. Put this idea to the test! Try the exercises below and record how you do. Then do them every few days to get better and better. After a month of practicing, fill out the next page and compare your results.

Date: ....

How many times can you jump rope without stopping? ....

How many push-ups can you do? ....

How high can you jump? ....
(Jump and touch a spot on the wall and then measure where you touched from the floor.)

How many jumping jacks can you do in one minute? ....

How many sit-ups can you do in one minute? ....

How long can you run in place without stopping? ....

How long can you keep a hula hoop spinning before it drops?

....

How many times can you bounce a soccer ball on your knee without

letting it hit the ground? ....

Date (after at least one month of exercising): ....

How many times can you jump rope without stopping? ....

How many push-ups can you do? ....

How high can you jump? ....

How many jumping jacks can you do in one minute? ....

How many sit-ups can you do in one minute? ....

How long can you run in place without stopping? ....

How long can you keep a hula hoop spinning before it drops?

....

How many times can you bounce a soccer ball on your knee without

letting it hit the ground? ....

List It

Put on your thinking cap! Create two lists about anything that interests you. (Among the endless possibilities, you have the tough choice of picking only two!)

Date: ....

List topic: ....

1. ....

2. ....

3. ....

4. ....

5. ....

6. ....

7. ....

8. ....

9. ....

10. ....

11. ....

Date: ....

List topic: ....

1. ....

2. ....

3. ....

4. ....

5. ....

6. ....

7. ....

8. ....

9. ....

10. ....

11. ....

The Future Me

On the left side, draw how you think you'll look in the future. On the right side, draw a picture of what your future life will look like. For example, answer these questions: Where will you live? Who will be a part of your family? Will you have pets? What kind of work will you do? How will you get from place to place? What will make you happy?

What year is it in your drawing? ....

Describe Your Day

Keep track of your activities and your feelings about this moment in time.

Date: ....

Today was a .... day.
(Fill in a word or phrase that best describes your day.)

What happened today: ....

....

....

....

....

How you feel about today: ....

....

What good things from today would you love to repeat?

....

....

....

....

What bad things from today would you choose to avoid?

What can you learn from today to make future days even better?

Dear Future Me

Use the space below to write a letter to your future self. What do you want to remember about who you are right now? What quality that you have now do you always want to keep?

Dear Future Me,

Love, Me at age

Dear Younger Me

Use the space below to write a letter to your younger self. What would you want the younger you to know? What would you say to your younger self that would make her excited about growing up?

Dear Younger Me,

_____

_____

_____

_____

_____

_____

_____

_____

Love, Me at age _____

Celebrate Yourself!

Fill the space below with doodles and words describing things you think are great about you. You're unique, and that is something to celebrate!

Write to us!
Send letters about why
you love being a girl to:

CKY2 *Journal* Editor
American Girl
8400 Fairway Place
Middleton, WI 53562

Here are some other American Girl books you might like:

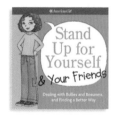